THE BIG SURPRISE

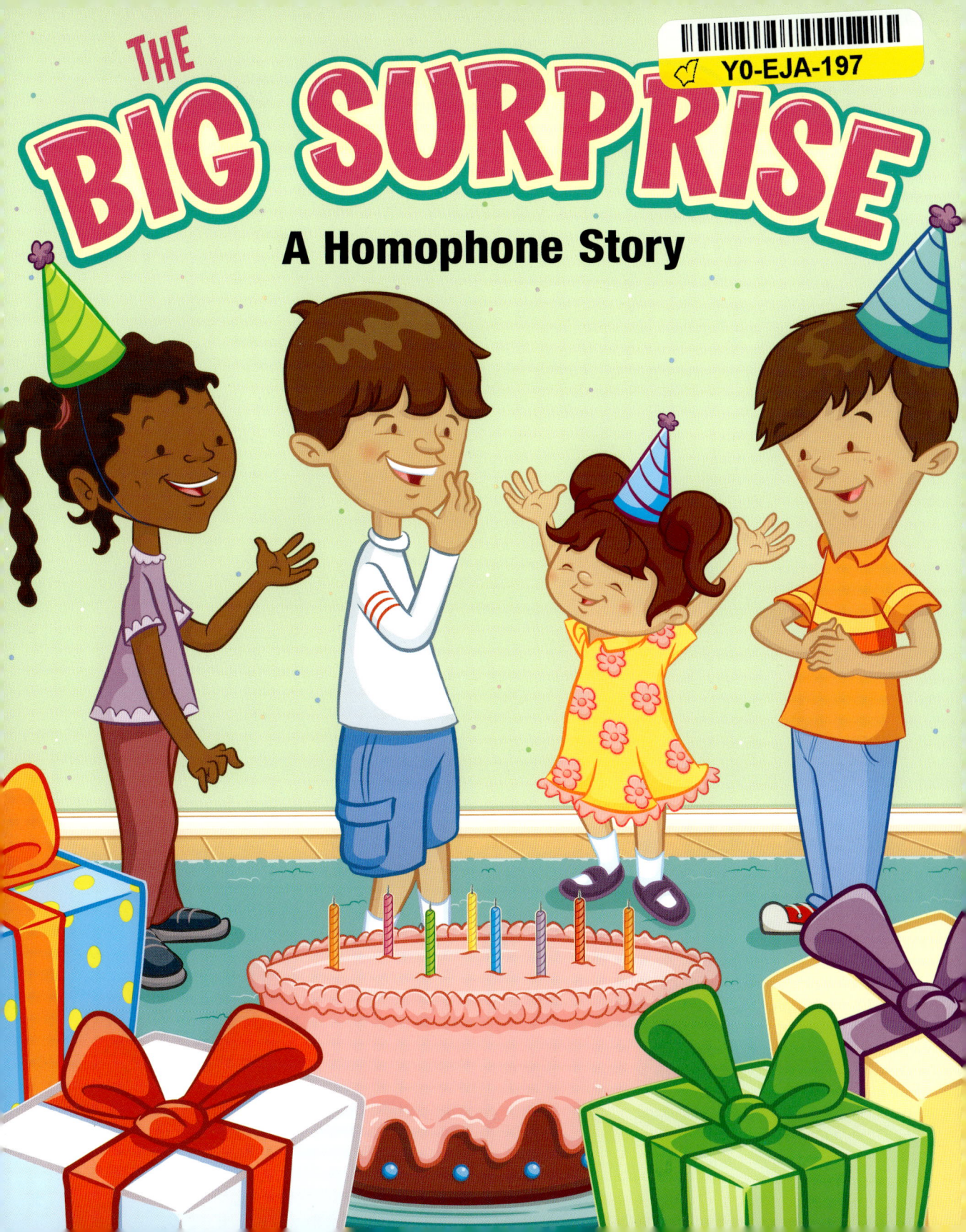

A Homophone Story

Derek and Erica had planned a surprise birthday party for their friend John. Now the big day was here!

"I can't wait until John can hear us all yell surprise!" said Derek. "It's going to be a great party."

"We better get the house ready," said Erica.

While Derek blew up a few balloons, Erica took out some large, blue paper. "Let's make some birthday signs to hang around the house," she said.

"Would you like to **choose** some crayons?" asked Erica. Derek gave her a funny look.

"No one **chews** crayons," he said. "That would make you sick."

Erica laughed. "I mean, would you like to pick some crayons?"

Derek laughed, too. They got crayons from the box.

Erica and Derek worked on their signs for an hour. "I think our signs are looking great!" Erica said.

Soon, they had eight different signs to hang around the house. Then, Erica remembered the cake.

"Let's make sure we hide the cake from your sister Sara so she won't eat it!" said Erica. "I remember on your last birthday she ate the cake before the party. We don't want that to happen again."

Erica taped the best birthday sign right on the mirror. Then, she and Derek hung the rest of the signs around the house.

Erica decided that she needed to make some more signs for one of the walls.

"What else can I write besides Happy Birthday? she asked Derek.

"Hope all your wishes come true!" Derek answered. Erica liked that, and she made two more signs.

Erica and Derek looked around the room and read all the signs they had made. Just then, Sara walked into the room. She was holding a crayon in each hand.

"Help?" she said.

"Sara wants to help with the party, too," said Erica.

"She's only two years old, but I guess she can help," said Derek.

Sara jumped up and down with excitement. Erica made one more sign and asked Sarah to color it red.

Soon, it was time to change clothes for the party. Sara wanted to wear her new yellow dress.

"Where is the dress? I can help her," said Erica.

Derek knew where it was. "It's in the laundry room," he said. "Be careful. The door sticks. If you close it all the way, you might not be able to get out."

Erica went to get the dress in the laundry room. Before she knew it, the door had closed. "Uh-oh!" said Erica, sounding scared.

She pushed on the door, but it wouldn't open. Then, the handle broke off!

Sara was on the other side of the door. She tried to pull it open but couldn't. She started to bawl loudly.

"Sara, don't cry. Go get Derek! He'll help us open the door," called Erica.

Sara stopped crying and left to find Derek, picking up her ball along the way.

Sara found Derek in the living room. He was wrapping his present for John and tying the ribbon in a knot.

"Go here," said Sara.

Derek was listening to music and did not hear Sara. She walked closer to him and tapped him on the shoulder.

Derek took off his headphones to see what Sara wanted.

"Go see," she said, pointing to the laundry room.

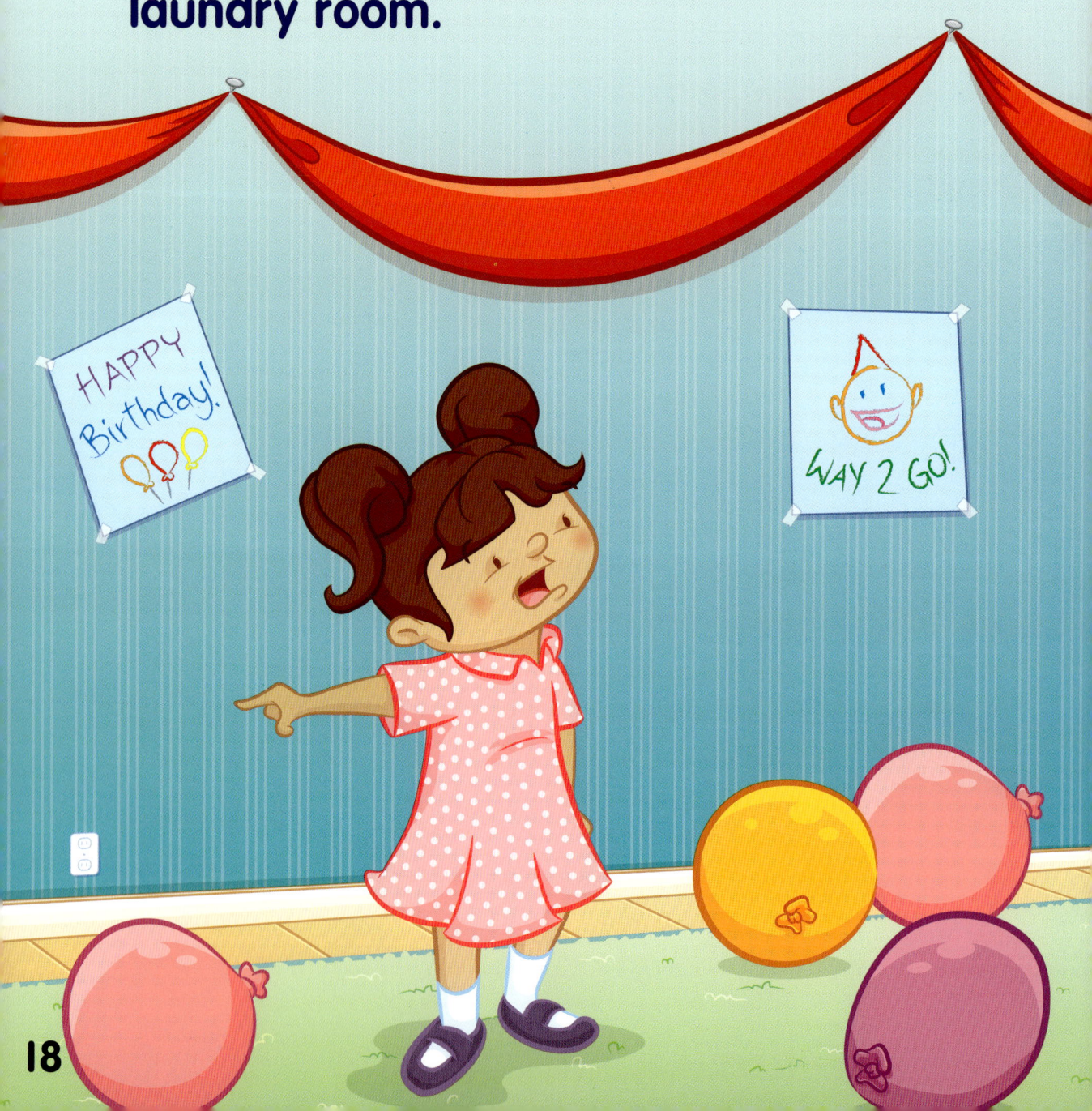

"We can't go to the sea, Sara," he said. "We'll go to the beach another day."

He turned around and began to hang streamers around the room.

Sara threw her arms in the air. She pulled Derek toward the laundry room. She pointed and said, "Erica!"

"Oh, now I understand!" said Derek at last. He and Sara pulled hard together and got the door open. Erica came *through* the door.

"Were you trying to get out of helping me or something?" Derek said with a laugh.

"Oh, that's so funny," Erica said. "At least I found a needle and thread in there. I had time to sew a loose button on Sara's dress."

Sara hugged Erica.

"You know, you didn't have to lock me down here, Sara. I would have fixed your dress anyway!" Erica joked.

Just then, Derek **heard** the doorbell ring. The guests arrived in a **herd** and began hiding. When John got **there**, they jumped out and yelled, "Happy birthday!" **Their** party was so much fun!